Planes

by Julie Murray

ABDO
TRANSPORTATION
Kids

www.abdopublishing.com

Published by Abdo Kids, a division of ABDO, PO Box 398166, Minneapolis, Minnesota 55439.

Copyright © 2015 by Abdo Consulting Group, Inc. International copyrights reserved in all countries.
No part of this book may be reproduced in any form without written permission from the publisher.

Printed in the United States of America, North Mankato, Minnesota.

052014

092014

Photo Credits: Shutterstock, Thinkstock,
© Christian Lagerek p.13, © Stanislaw Tokarski p.15 / Shutterstock.com

Production Contributors: Teddy Borth, Jennie Forsberg, Grace Hansen

Design Contributors: Candice Keimig, Laura Rask, Dorothy Toth

Library of Congress Control Number: 2013953009

Cataloging-in-Publication Data

Murray, Julie.

 Planes / Julie Murray.

   p. cm. -- (Transportation)

ISBN 978-1-62970-080-9 (lib. bdg.)

Includes bibliographical references and index.

1. Airplanes--Juvenile literature.   I. Title.

629.133--dc23

                2013953009

Table of Contents

Planes

Planes fly in the sky. They move people from place to place.

Many people travel by
planes. They are used
all over the world.

Parts of a Plane

The front of the plane is called the **nose**. The back is called the **tail**.

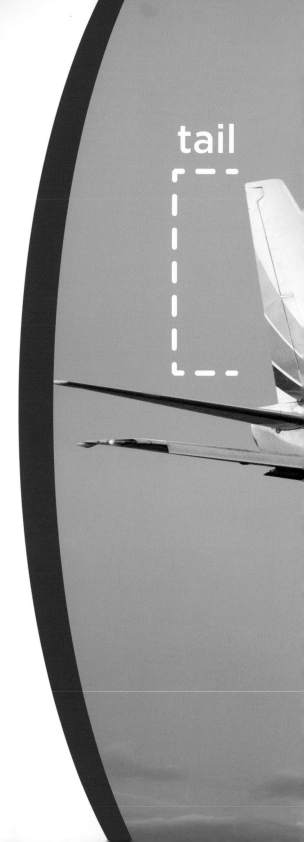

tail

nose

Pilots sit in the **cockpit**.

Computers help pilots

fly the plane.

11

The plane's **hold** is on the bottom. This is where the luggage is kept.

13

People sit in the cabin.

There are seats, TVs,

and bathrooms here.

Engines power the plane.

Wings help them fly.

17

Planes take off and land on a **runway**. They have wheels to move on the ground.

19

Airports

People get on and off planes at an airport. Airports are full of people traveling all over the world.

21

More Facts

- A plane lands every three seconds somewhere in the world.

- The first time a plane was flown successfully was by the Wright brothers on December 17, 1903.

- Air travel is the safest form of travel.

Glossary

cockpit – a space in the front of an airplane. The cockpit holds the controls and seats for the pilot and copilot.

hold – the belly of the plane that holds the cargo. Cargo can be anything from mail, to goods, to suitcases.

nose – the front of the plane.

runway – a long strip on which planes take off and land.

tail – the back part of the plane.

Index

abdokids.com

Use this code to log on to abdokids.com and access crafts, games, videos and more!

Abdo Kids Code:
TPK0809

6113478